AN AUSTRALIAN PRESIDENTS MANIFESTO (MODEL CONSTITUTION)

(to update; work in progress ; to improve and complete).

2023 December 18th update.

By: Loris Hemlof.

---- THE NATIONAL CONSTITUTION OF AUSTRALIA;

The Presidents Manifesto (Candidate to become the Australian Constitution) shall arise from written model Australian Government Presidents Manifesto submission from any male Australian citizen born in Australia of 10generations ancestry all white, orange, red blend skin, black, grey or yellow hair and blue, green or brown eyes; Selection of the leading manifesto and president by optional preferential vote; a voluntary vote modifiable during each year; of 1000 member citizens jury, 100 forming the upper house of each of the 10states and to also function as the federal Australian Parliaments Senate; by random selection of citizens jury from asset poor (having total assets of less than GDP per capita) of fair skin ancestry;

50males and 50females; over the age of 15 years and born in each state, who self nominate with no exclusions because of criminal record, bias or conflict of interest. Teleconferencing of citizens jury sessions across the 10 state upper house citizens juries of the Australian states and broadcast to populace. The author of the winning manifesto submission shall become the President for each year; the President having the choice to provide assent to legislation if moving towards compliance with his winning Australian Government Charter. If the President resigns or has died the successor shall be the Presidents choice of vice President to provide assent but in compliance with the Presidents manifesto.

The joint votes of 10state 100member Citizens Jury shall also elect a Governor General every year; to write military doctrine and the broad defence budget. The current Governor General may Pardon at the rate of 1 each day. Plus the Governor General shall confirm the coalition to be the government and the Prime Minister and Prime Minister's ministry including Treasurer from the prime ministers nominations. Ministers shall be from members of the lower house the House of Common

Representatives; The Prime Minister's Treasurer shall present the national Government budget and ministers shall present spending to the House of Common Representatives for vote subject to the citizens jury and the Presidents assent subject to reversal within one year of assent. The Governor General shall have such powers such as to appoint Military and Emergency services personnel and replace government personnel (including where in office by election but not disqualify the citizens jury).

The 10 states of Australia shall be; New South Wales and Australian Capital Territory, Victoria, Queensland, South Australia, South West Australia, North West Australia, Tasmania, Northern Territory, North Island of New Zealand, and the South Island of New Zealand.

Prior laws of any parliament shall continue to apply until enactment of new legislation. Prior laws shall be void as much as were inconsistent with current newer laws. All other international agreements and membership of international organisations such as courts shall be void.

National legislative power shall reside with the national Parliament, which shall consist of the will of the fair populace, The Prime Minister ministers, the House of Representatives, the state Citizens Juries, the Governor General and the President.

Qualification of Candidates,Voters, Educators, Party members, Governor General, Governor, Jury, Student scholarships, Populace affordable housing tenants, Representatives by election and appointment and Members of the populace service; shall all be fair ancestry full citizens born in the electorate and having less total assets than GDP per capita. Qualification for the public service shall exclude people of dark complexion, migrants, homosexuals, criminals, and asset rich.

Male valid voters in general elections shall have 1 compulsory vote (except where disabled and not able to get to a poling place) vote from the age of enrolling to vote over the age or 15years, Female valid voters shall have 1 compulsory vote for each dependant; for husband and for each genetic child including pregnancy up to the age of the child enrolling to vote on own behalf when over the age of 15years. The ballot shall be in person at polling place at any day time during election week; by presenting identification and submitting to a photograph on election week at one local polling place; Image recognition shall eliminate fraud. Elections shall have optional preferential voting. Every 2 years on the election week holiday from 15th April full citizens shall vote at official polling booth for national, state and local council elections.

Public servants and political parties shall receive no pay from the Australian government budgets or be bribed during term/s of administration (only normal work for assets test welfare of the citizen populace and party membership fees).

Presidential Estate Funding: .9% of the national government budget shall be for the Presidential estate to pay for upkeep of Presidential estate properties. Presidential estate income, properties and inheritance shall be tax free. Also 9% of the Presidential estate budget shall be for housing on the Presidential personal estate for descendants of fallen or wounded fair patriots who have died in action defending Australia and of siblings descendants if the fallen patriot did not have children.

Provision for the Governor General: The President may direct and assent to the Governor Generals Presidential estate budget.

The Governor General shall direct Presidential estate budget to fund the Presidential electoral boundaries commission to determine electoral boundaries. The Governor General may determine local, state, and national electoral and court jurisdiction boundaries; so Australia will each have 10 states each with 10 local council areas, each of as equal as possible (population x land area in hectares), also considering natural boundaries such as of big islands.

Sitting sessions of Parliament and Local council assemblies: Members of Parliament shall attend an over 40 hour week (Monday to Friday); in session the first two whole weeks each month. Members may teleconference and vote remotely; with video monitor in each corner of the parliament chamber; for remote members with the Speaker having a button to control when hearing the remote members microphone. The Prime Minister, Premier and Mayor may determine extra sittings and sitting extensions. The Governor General may also have an assembly sit and end sitting. Members of parliament (national, states and local councils) may not go overseas. International agreements are void.

National parliament House of Representatives; fair citizens to elect 200 members of the House of Representatives; in each of the 10 states; each of the 10 local councils area electorates elect 1 male fair citizens and 1 female fair citizen both born in the electorate; For twenty members from each state. Full citizens of Australia born in the electorate; may nominate for party preselection election by electorate born party members; for election to parliament and local council.

Each state parliament lower house the house of assembly; shall by election elect 5 male and 5 female members for each of the 10 local council areas; for a total of 100 members of each state parliament lower house; the house of assembly.

Each local council area shall elect 5 fair males and 5 fair females to the local council by postal vote. For a total of 10 members of each local council.

Local council areas are local courts jurisdiction areas.

 A 50% +1 vote majority (over half of all members including who were absent) of the house of representatives of the national parliament plus of the citizens jury of the 10 states 100 members (for a total of 1,000 members) of the shall pass legislation and budget. This number shall include the speaker only where to carry motions in the chamber. The party room may update regulation as the minister may put with over 50%+ of votes of ruling coalition members of the house of common representatives of parliament. Each regulation shall be up to 1x A4 page of size 14 font text. For a over all total of up to 700 pages of regulation in total in addition to budgets each of which may be up to 70 pages. 20% of the total members of the the chamber of parliament or council may enforce splitting of bills into individual items.

 The Governor Generals Australian broad defence budget and doctrine statement and state ministers spending submissions subject to be within national budget allocation in having approval of parliament and not rejection by the states Citizens Juries. All for products and services made by local industry in own nation so support local industry development.

Imprisonment of every member of parliament in parliament until producing a budget to actually result in a surplus.

No laws in relation to crimes; a random jury of 9 fair unrelated willing citizens shall determine all penalties on the merits of the individual case.

Permanent vacancy by notification, vacancy, absence, crimes or illness: Whenever an elected representative permanent vacancy happens as the Governor General shall determine after the speaker (chair) of the house of representatives notifies the Governor General. The replacement shall be by same party member postal branch selection.

Each of the 10 largest parties by membership may appoint a scrutineer at each polling place where shall count votes.

Oath or affirmation of allegiance: Every member of the House of Representatives and every member of a state parliament and local council, shall before taking seat make and subscribe before the Governor General, an oath or affirmation of allegiance to a fair Australia.

Resignation of a member: A member may by address the Speaker of the chamber and present the Speaker with a written resignation, the relevant state Governor may accept a resignation letter for confirmation.

The Governor General to determine the Governing coalition having most valid members of the House Of Representatives.

A valid person may only have appointment to one house of Parliament.

Electors must register and update permanent address. Voting is compulsory for valid voters with fine of 1% of weekly earnings income while having failed to lodge valid vote except where incapacitated. The Governor General's Court may resolve disputed elections.

Absence of a speaker (chair of the chamber): After 5 minutes in a session sitting without a speaker in the speaker's chair including any of the 3 deputies; the chamber may elect to approve a member of the chamber to become the new deputy speaker (chair). The Governor General may also determine the chamber replace and ban a member from being speaker of the chamber. The speaker of the chamber may also resign by verbal address to the chamber and also by writing to the Governor General with verbal confirmation such as by phone. Speakers (chairs) rules and orders for the chamber: The speaker of each chamber of an assembly of populace servants having election may update the powers, privileges, rules and immunity of the members of the chamber, the mode in which its powers, privileges, and immunity may be exercised and upheld subject to Presidential veto. A member of parliament or local council may lodge with the speaker; written request for temporary absence and name a valid proxy member from the same chamber for up to 2 months absence with the speakers approval then confirmation. Failed attendance of members to the chamber: The chamber may proceed with business even if members have failed to arrive for the session from 10am on session days; until adjournment by more than 50% of attending members by vote. If a count is disputed any member may call for a division; the ringing of the signal bells with green light for House of Representatives and signal bell throughout the national Parliament for 4 minutes or also after the leader in the chamber of the Prime

Ministers Government calls for adjournment. Each hour of debate shall be of a subject of the choosing of each member of the house of parliament or council in full rotation. The call shall go to a members on request having least speaking time in last week alternating the call between the government and an opposition member. Quorum: More than 40% of the members by election of the chamber must be in the chamber for a quorum so debate may proceed. More than 150 valid members must be in the chamber for a valid vote quorum after ringing signal bell with red light throughout the national parliament. Attendance of more members than who vote on the bill in the chamber within 1 month may have the chamber vote again on the bill.

Communications. Black complexion people or homosexuals may not be heard. Video security surveillance shall monitor and record silent video of all public places to catch crime including public toilets. Government may not own media or schools.

RADIO SPECTRUM: All radio spectrum is free. Government may not sell or charge rent for spectrum. As set by the national parliament:

{Device transmitting under 100 Milliwatt may use any spectrum without limit, restriction or cost, up to 10 MHz per user allowing devices to switch to unused frequencies, Except may not use GPS, radar, navigation, emergency, and missile guidance spectrum up to 100mhz. Radio Quiet Zone: {} to a radius of {} shall have no radio emissions except in emergencies for radio telescope. *25khz from 0khz to 25khz military submarine communications. *25khz from 25 kHz to 50 kHz positioning system. *25khz from 50 kHz to 200 kHz over the horizon radar. *29.8mhz from 200 kHz to 20mhz national digital radio station broadcasts. *20mhz to 150mhz open channel two way radio free of fee or license open use. *150mhz to 250mhz city wide radio station broadcasts [DAB+] *250mhz to 10ghz mobile phone, internet and wireless local networking; towers, satellite and wireless router. Fee sharing of towers and portion of backbone fibre bandwidth in proportion to distance of unique standard backbone fibre rolling out. Reserving from this spectrum requirements standard spectrum for global positioning systems, microwave ovens, and radar. *5 GHz spectrum from 10 GHz to 15 GHz satellite educational television. *60ghz from

15 to 75 GHz for rural satellite dish internet. *5 GHz spectrum from 75 GHz to 80 GHz; Airport radar channels. *20 GHz spectrum from 80 GHz to 100 GHz free open vehicle radar spectrum such as for robot AI taxi bus and AI autopilot drones with self navigation and backup video path mapping so not collide or stray. To 10 watts emitter subject to local council settings. *Spectrum 10ghz from 100 GHz to 110ghz for radio telescopes. *Spectrum over 110ghz open spectrum..

 Standards including technologies to be free to copy. Text and image copyrights, Product design and medication patents (when a product is the standard the makers and designers must make the technologies of operation and construction openly available and free to copy), All genetics may not be patented and are free to copy subject to therapy, hygiene, pest control, contraception such as in infections for genocide (of terrorist races such as blacks) and correction of bad genes).

 Business: Each of the 10 largest shareholders who are individual full citizens born in Australia shall each have only 1 directorship in the local business and company.

The justice process including rewards from the national budget for evidence leading to convictions. The local council panel of 2 judges and 9 unrelated fair (white orange red) complexion jurists together shall vote by 5 and more majority votes to select sentence proposition of 1 of the 2 judges. 50% of compensation for the victim and 50% for lawyer.

Laws, records, plans and judicial process by agreement of State premiers to have recognition throughout Australia.

The national parliament shall legislate to discriminate against people of black complexion and for people of fair complexion. Genocide of pest species or dark complexion races may only by control of fertility, such as sterilisation contraception by injection and by providing good food aid. Only black complexion biological parents have the right to free abortion and in exchange for aid. Including for foreign starved refugees. Blacks shall also retain their natural right to savage each other on their black native title area nations (Papua New Guinea) and prison islands. Children may only reside with people of own race so not stolen. Only fair (white orange red) complexion born full citizens of more than 95% fair (white orange red) ancestry on all lineages for 1000 years and who are born in Australia and over the age of 20 years may Vote, Have the right to run as a candidate for election; Be in the public service (including by election); Be in public housing (as service providers and as tenants); Be in our homeland security militia and forces (NATO alliance forces may visit subject to our Governor General who may also employ foreigner or if of dark complexion in military including abroad); and Fair full citizen men over the age of 50 years who have done no crime to age of 50 years shall also have the default right to own, carry and use a long gun anywhere on own land, home and vehicle with stand your ground legal defence for to use the standard firearm against those who have violated the man's property, and as fair full citizen females shall have the right to carry a handgun with laser pointer to aim and kill black savages with rape panic legal defence. Citizens with legal authority to carry a firearm may do so on own property or where having official authorisation of state governor, and governor general for the nation of Australia; such as private security police and militia.

The national parliament shall have power to make laws over external affairs: the President may exit any international agreement and continue to make new laws independent of any international agreement without penalty, (Parliament not compelled or be subjected to foreign laws or agreements). Regulation of transport within the lands, seas and airs of Australia; Providers of mandatory drivers insurance shall determine and issue driver's licenses. Unions shall manage fair worker health and safety and proper payment for employment, may withdrawal labour, services and component products. Courts may prosecute unions if extorted wages which were unfair. Minimum wage per hour for compulsory work for otherwise unproductive assets test welfare recipients; average home prices / 18,000 [$50per hour]. The maximum wage for an employee of an organisation is 20x the average wage for the organisation; share options may not be paid as wages. Public service including members of parliament not subject to minimum wage, public service to work for free as the minister shall employ by mutual agreement. Charity workers, parties, unions, police, military, populace servants, members of parliament and ministers may not be bribed or have negotiated to be bribed such as with lucrative easy jobs after leaving office. Members of parliament, Ministers, and the Governor General may continue usual commercial business having when gaining office so as to encourage complementary interests with industry. Only small political parties may only accept donations from fair full citizens of Australia and only as a charity up to where having 5 members of state and national parliaments and local councils, with 6 and more members of state and national parliaments and of local council chambers, the parties revenue may only be equal portion of the state the state and national parliament and local council budget surplus in proportion to the standing votes of members who are sitting members of parliament on the passing of the next broad budget. Government ministers shall consider additional matters as the President determines. Terms of reform of State constitution, legislation, and local government by the Parliament and citizens of each State subject to the Presidents manifesto. The national parliament may legislate regulation to further define laws, penalties, levies and taxes in regulations of up to 1 page with a total of up to 700 pages subject to assent of the Governor General, regulations which any future Prime Minister may annul. Local fuels and finite resources. The national parliament may set a minimum percentage of each producer miners finite fuels and essential mining resources production which shall be for supply of local consumers including industry in Australia. Additional rights and privileges for good fair full citizens and responsibilities and obligations of guest residents migrants. Powers of the national national Parliament and in respect of legislation (subject to the Presidents manifesto): to make laws for the peace, order, and good government of Australia; Laws to spend revenue and direct levies (to useful purposes for the earner to choose) and impose and regulate taxation and fine (so have penalty from that to dissuade) and fees (to control and filter), shall originate in the House Of Representatives only as with the Prime Ministers Treasurers broad national budget for national revenue. Local council area courts consist of 2 judges; 1 from each of the 2 parties with most members of parliament, plus 9 jurists by voluntary willing self nomination then by random selection. The Governor General may regulate the Governor General's Tribunal and provide assent to each determination including each penalty; The citizens jury may not amend bill, So shall originate from the Prime Ministers relevant minister in the House Of Representatives so comply to the Prime Ministers Treasurer's budget also to originate in the House of Representatives. The citizens jury may vote to return a bill to the House of Representatives without amendment with a message of up to 1 page requesting amendments and omissions in relation to the bill. And the relevant Minister in the House Of Representatives may consider and amend the bill until the House of Representatives vote in approval for return to the national citizens jury to vote on.

Powers of Prime Minister: Members gaining election to the House of Representatives voting with a coalition where winning a majority in a vote of confidence after election shall on the request of the Governor General form the ruling government and each member of the national parliament shall have 2 votes for separate members from any voluntary candidates from within the coalition to become the Prime Minister who may while Prime Minister create, merge and dissolve departments so determine number, so appoint and replace each government minister and deputy minister from the valid members by election of the House in the coalition with the duties of each ministers in the House of Representatives including the Treasurer who shall present the budget with budget statements, for each minister to prepare relevant legislation for approval of both houses, and then call for project spending submissions for approval of the minister and then the national Citizens Jury. The Prime Minister and Ministers shall be within 100 km of the national parliament sitting on rotation each year in each state parliament, subject to the Governor General determination determination of general rotation and emergency alternatives. Ordinary members having election to Parliament may attend Parliament chamber from own electorate via a video monitors in the corners of each chamber of parliament and to lodge votes to the Parliament electronically and securely as with all members of the house for live online verification by anyone in the world. The Treasurers broad budget from having voluntary line item assent of the Governor General shall go before the House of Representatives and states Citizens Juries (voting as 1x 1000 member jury). Tax bills: In compliance with the Treasurers annual broad budget; Each law creating, modifying or abolishing a tax including a fee, fine and levy including the rate shall be an individual and separate bill originating with the relevant Minister in the House Of Representatives and shall only deal with the one tax measure, additional parts shall be void but shall not void the tax measure bill. Spending bills: Each spending submission to spend revenue (money) on 1 A4 page with normal text and illustrations shall each only deal with one item of purchase, the spending submission shall not exceed the revenue as a percentage total revenue in compliance with the Treasurers annual broad budget. Subject to final assent from the President which the President may reverse within one year. Presidential assent to Bills: When a bill (law) passes both chambers of the Parliament, the President may provide assent subject to this Australian Government Charter, which the President may reverse within one year. With denial of assent the President may return the bill to the originator member and recommend in general amendments for the bill. The bill with compliant amendments may then return to the parliament for votes. Dis-allowance by the President: Allocation to the Governor Generals for broad defence spending shall go to the Australian national parliament for management by the nations defence and aid minister.

The President may also provide a Presidential Pardon to an individual each week.

 The Executive Government; Executive power: The executive power of Australia is vested in the President to lend assent to new laws of Australian parliaments, Appoint state governors to lend assent to state parliaments and local council. The Governor General to command, authorise, appoint and replace all police, emergency services, military forces and defend Australia and Australian Government Charter update having approval of more than 50% of citizens jurists of the Australia and legislation having Presidential signature for Presidential assent. National Executive Council: The Governor General shall choose and update a national Executive Council to ask for advice and information about governance of Australia and may summon to and host voluntary meetings of the national Executive and reward members who attend. The President may reappoint and replace leaders and personnel including government ministers and populace servants, military and police, Plus of charities with accreditation of a government, These personnel replacements may serve to end of the term of employment up to 5 years subject to Presidential alteration and be members of the national Executive Council. The President may also create, modify, privatise and abolish government departments with personnel. The Presidents national Parliament minister replacement may hold office for up to three months then the Prime Minister may select a minister from members having election to the relevant chamber of national Parliament. Number of Ministers: As the number of members in the coalition gaining election allow The Prime Minister may have any number of ministers in the House of Common Representatives. The Prime Minister's ministers having election to the House of Representatives and appointment to the relevant department may oversee and direct selection, replacement and duties of populace servants subject to interventions of the President or Governor General (military, law enforcement, border protection, aid and emergency services).

The Governor General being in ultimate command of the Australian military, time travel, security police, militia and humanitarian aid forces; As the command in chief to delegate authorisation of all naval and military forces in the lands, airspace to 100 km and waters of Australia. Transfer of certain departments: The President on the Prime Ministers advice may transfer government departments to another Parliament including Local Councils in Australia and privatise government corporations services and infrastructure to compete in the private and charity sectors, with continuation of pay of the populace servants as employees of the private businesses and charities to earn more than the minimum wage for each hour of manual work for 10 years at the same location. Extra powers of Governors to vest in Governor General: The Australian national parliament may legislate to offer extra voluntary powers but not obligations to the Governor General.

The Judiciary: Local Courts: Each Local Council shall have a Local Court to adjudicate over all crimes which happened closest to it. On conviction each of 2 Judges shall submit a penalty, each of the 9 Jurists shall then have 1 vote to cast to 1 of the 2 separate Judges penalty submission. The penalty having the most jurist votes shall apply, for Judges penalty submissions having equal votes the convict may choose between these penalties. Convicts may appeal to the President for Presidential Pardon, being up to pardon of up to 1 individual person each week. In addition a 30 year statute of limitations shall apply on all crimes of over 30 years before subject to confession including for claims by black aboriginals, so claims of land rights by black aboriginals for alleged crimes done by settlers in ancient times are void. Obtaining justice shall be free, lawyers must provide services for free with pay only from a legal aid charity having accreditation to receive donations. Witness including the victim shall receive equal reward for evidence leading to each conviction each month from 1% of the national defence budget for division equally between each of the 100 local councils for the local court/s each month as compensation and rewards for afflicted for convictions subject to state governor veto of the reward within one month.

Black or native ancestry and black citizens born in Australia may get release of prison without welfare to reside on native title prison islands pending deportation. Blacks born in our nation shall resettle in independent native title nation (Papua New Guinea) the government to receive financial aid. Also to process illegals who have invaded Australia to return to nation(s) of genetic ancestry (subject to DNA test) regardless of rejected by that country.

 The Governor General may establish, regulate and appoint and determine terms for investigators, prosecutors and Judges for each Governor Generals Tribunals with verdicts and penalties subject to Governor General assent. The Governor General may have a Governor Generals Tribunal investigate any matter particularly of government if corrupted or disqualified or war crimes done by any personnel within areas of our government and military jurisdiction including in foreign nations whose government by election invites us in alliance coalition to help defend; So not be convicted by our Local Courts. Plus may investigate if was injustice on advice of the Prime Minister. Appeal to the President for Presidential Pardon and also for Referral for (re)-adjudication by voluntary vote by all citizens jurist; The Australian President may provide 1 Presidential Pardon each week for 1 for full citizen residing anywhere the Australian law may have influence, these pardons shall include foreigners the Australian border protection minister shall choose to exile and banish. The Presidential Pardon shall remove and compensate for if wrongly convicted and return confiscated property and fine; This compensation from the agency who wrongly prosecuted shall by GDP divide by population divide by 100 [$700] for each day the wrongly imprisoned or detained and exempt the fair born full citizen from being similarly prosecuted or limited by any person, force, court and tribunal within Australian jurisdiction and reach and require protection for any similar activity by the fair born citizen so as to be able to continue similar activities subject to annulment by the President. (This 1 Presidential Pardon each week for 1 fair born citizen shall also apply to where living abroad). Local Courts may impose a penalty if solitary incarceration for free in private cell with temperature moderation, shower, toilet and basin with drinking fountain, built in bed with bedding and only true images of self and on television. With provision of food, cleaning and medication needs (convicts may do cleaning to earn good behaviour concessions). If the sentence of confinement shall be for more than one year, and one year since the last crime receiving extension of sentence of confinement and one month since damaged self or was addicted to drugs or smoked the care home may release the patient or for convicts the prison shall have the local court review a convicts sentence of confinement. Convicts must have own room with own bathroom. Convicts may earn an amount of pay for work as the person is willing so have some freedom or if was not willing let rest in solitary in own room. For convicts on parole free to roam and live on the prison parole island for the remainder of the sentence unless convicted by the Local Court for a crime with a penalty of a term of solitary confinement again with some freedom for productive convict work. Full citizens addicted to recreational drugs shall resettle on a prison island in state public housing if poor in assets, where may roam free within the coasts of the prison islands free to grow drugs which intoxicated. The prison island operator charity to provide vitals including citizens 3 free welfare ration optimal nutrition bars each day, plus may pay any amount for manual labour when worth while. Addicted shall have detention in private hospital room until after 1 year free of drugs. The national parliament lower first House border protection minister shall determine assessment of foreigners and probationary citizenship holders for detention for deportation if have done crimes of over 1 month in prison, been infected with a lethal infection or run up GDP/population [$70,000] in medical debts; criminal defence lawyers may not appeal and any suit of behalf of foreigner may not be heard in any court. So enforcement of deportation to the migrants home country of foreign citizenship or main ancestry more than 500 years ago after confinement subject to the death penalty for repeated savagery or illegally re entered and as additional punishment including to face death penalty from the foreigners own people. Final jurisdiction of Governor Generals Tribunal and Australian Citizens Juries in council in all matters regardless of law or treaty; Appointment of Local Court Judges and Jurists: Each Local Court room shall have a panel seating 2 judges each of the 2 parties having most members of parliament in the nation from candidates from party members born in the local council area who shall elect a locally born and resident member to be Judge in the Local Court until retirement as the Governor General may determine. Each local court shall have 10 jurists from local born able fair citizen local resident over the age of 20 years of age who voluntarily apply for 1 year, each for random appointment as one of 10 Jurists one month in advance for one year and substitutes for if any unable to attend. Indictment or any offence against any local court shall be by jury, and every such trial shall be held in the Local Court of the local council area where the offence was committed or the local court nearest to the crime shall hear. Local Council shall approve private security police force subject to the state Governor to arrest criminals until a local judge determines remand and bail terms and date for court appearance the event of multiple judges the higher restriction shall apply. Local Court conviction shall by by preferential vote of 9 jurists voting on sentencing submissions of 2 local court judges. Fair Security Police Officer including border protection shall be able to arrest and deport blacks or illegal invader without access to courts, Send intoxicated, addicts, psychotic or self harmed to hospital detention, and Confine assailants including for illegal supply of drug or intoxicated drivers for trial. Fair security police officers may shoot in defence of fair citizens; black terrorists or fugitive murderers. Segregation of criminals in jail shall be national on basis of gender, race, age and type of crime. All prisoners shall have right to segregation in own cell for own protection and hygiene plus air conditioning for temperature control plus good nutrition and health care. All criminals as prisoners shall have sterilisation by a injection after 1 year in prison (cumulative). Worst repeated violent criminals or illegal drug dealers shall have the death penalty at the rate of 1% of criminal prisoners each year. The border protection may deport foreigners who are criminals such as illegals to face death. Tax agents shall receive 1% of tax collection. No obligation on anybody to lodge tax forms. Equal (area in hectares x population) budget total portion for each of 10 states. Electricity generation shall be local as much as is possible. All homes shall be single story (except for state capitals city square mile). All communications, banking and energy systems shall be able to survive x60 electromagnetic storms. Payment to suppliers shall be in advance of supply (escrow), on supply the buyer may release payment, or after a period in the agreement the purchaser may recover amounts in escrow. Ministers may choose and dismiss staff and public servants in the department subject to approval of the Prime Minister.

Secession: States may not secede unless on a separate land mass area (island) or with own predominate other language by 60% majority referendum of full fair citizens with 100+ year ancestry (adding together lineages) on that land mass or language area in the last 200 years. Inconsistency of laws: The law of a State shall apply except where inconsistent with a law of the national national parliament, in which case the national parliament law shall prevail, and the former shall, to the extent of the inconsistency, be void. States and the national government may both enforce border protection; monitor, catch, apprehend, punish and deport immediately illegal blacks who have invaded or terrorised the state even if having obtained citizenship. All intoxicants are illegal; except may only be grown on island for addicted. Charities donations to receive tax exemption where having approval of the local council, but charities including religions workers not exempt from the minimum wage. Postal service franchise may offer banking services. Merchants selling from Australia may only accept the official national currency. Financial debts of Australian Governments shall be void at the end of each year. No fee or obstacle may be put on early payment, change of address and transfer between service providers. Rental bonds are illegal; a landlord may increase in rent if property damaged; to only pay when not evicted. The state may rent out forever properties left vacant for 1 year, with payment of rent to the owner after maintenance expenses. Compulsory acquisition of vacant blocks, derelict buildings, farming land at GDP / population / 10 [$5,000] per hectare to subdivide and sell at market price. Banks may issue replacement currency for currency damaged or destroyed. Any individual bill issuer to have own individual billing number from the account holder may be blocked at any time by the account holder. All bank and investments account holders must nominate beneficiaries accounts to transfer deposits to after account dormant for 5 years.

BUSINESSES AND SHARE MARKETS: Banks shall register (subject to criminal record check) any personal business with a unique company name not elsewhere used in the last 50 years taking up to 1 day for approval. 36% of after tax profit of listing business shall go to buy back (if each share trading below intrinsic value per share) or dividend (if each share trading above intrinsic value per share) pay out in direct account payments of 1% yield to each share for the shareholders. 36% of after tax profit of listing business shall go to equal per hour yearly bonus to employees working for the employer more than 100hours in the year. Business may never de-list from an official share market and may never be removed from listing on the same share market while in existence. Each entity may own up to 18% of listing companies: Take overs are illegal but assets may be sold. All businesses listing in Australia shall have 10 directors, each a full citizen of this nation (after 15 years probationary residency) with each of the 10 largest shareholder by ordinary shares each appoint and replace 1 director. All derivatives or financial instruments where the shareholder has not own the underlying business asset or having the potential for more than

100% loss of the cash investment are illegal and void. Foreigners may only own up to 1 hectare of land and where to commission building construction or where to be first resident after construction. Bankruptcy and insolvency (1 year as convict after payment for other crimes shall forgive bankruptcy and all financial and material debts);

 TRADE WITHIN THE 10 STATES; shall be free, except in matters of state customs controls for quarantine and prevention of entry of criminals or illegal foreign migrants or illegal weapons or illegal drugs. The national parliament shall give equal preference by equal land area x population between the states or any part thereof; by any law or expenditure. Laws with respect to navigation, or shipping, airlines, and railway carriers shall be made by the national parliament. The private national letter delivery monopoly must home deliver to homes and businesses in Australia for a basic single amount per letter up to 100grams. Parcel delivery is unregulated. The populace democratic national Parliament may ban any religion only to protect religious diversity such as to ban any religion that has abused or terrorised religions, including all books, places of worship or symbols and jailing and expulsion of their fanatics. Our parliaments and local councils may each legislate additional rules and observances without ceding power to any other religion. Good productive fair full citizens shall have free will to create own religion, observance and model policy submissions. Books and preaching of religion shall include metaphorical analogy to demonstrate moral principles, subject to correction by the living leader of the religion to be non fiction in light of the progress of science.

[model] NATIONAL BUDGET:

TAXATION:

 36% tariff on all currency leaving Australia, (such as on shifted profits to tax havens so avoided tax, or to buy imported products). On sale of cryptocurrency. All proceeds of a fair market price for of product exports must return into the Australian national currency within an Australian bank within 30 days of receipt, or pay a 36% tax on overseas revenue: Transport movements exempt.

 1.8% levy on corporate sales and revenue for the earners choices of free private selective schools for 5 to 15years of age educational television, .

1.8% levy on corporate sales and revenue for the earners choices of free private, technical colleges, on the job skills coach, video on demand online video library and employment services. No other taxes on profits or consumption sales.

18% levy on personal income including welfare from government for health and welfare savings superannuation contributions; to draw down for welfare at rate of .9% of savings each month.

9% tax on shares sales and dividends for collection by the platform.

72% capital gains tax on sale of used real estate including land. New unused real estate exempt, first sale of subdivision lots less than 1 hectare exempt. For payment from proceeds of sale. (commercial builders exempt so no tax on new construction)(no annual land or housing tax).

.9% levy on all income and revenue for the sellers choices of private emergency services company; having approval of the Governor General; Private border protection, police, fire fighters, rescue, disaster help, video surveillance cameras and military; using homeland defence minister budget for military and emergency services hardware.

Vacant land less than 1 hectare tax equal to 36% of the standard assets test welfare.

Vacant bedroom tax equal to 36% of the standard assets test welfare divided by the number of bedrooms in the dwellings.

For audit; .09% levy on business, charity and party revenue for audit;

A tax on each gram of sugar, sodium chloride salt or unhealthy oils in a product of GDP/population then / 10million. [.8cents per gram]

Resource export royalties : 36% tax on the export of natural resources; ores, gas, oil, precious stones, natural forest sourced timber and wild ocean sourced sea life exports. To pay once (may come and go free after paying export royalty once). No tax on the export of materials such as steel, ingots, bars, cut stones, components and final product. Land owners including aboriginals do not have the right to extort royalties.

Death tax of 72% of world wide wealth over (GDP / population) x 180 [$9million], at death of people born in Australia. Inheritance; the oldest homeless male genetic descendant including nephews of the deceased shall inherit the husbands family home and estate.

 Wealth tax of 9% of world wide wealth over (GDP / population) x 180 [$9million] each year; of people born in Australia.

 72% tax on gifts over GDP / population then x 9 [$500,000] each year to each entity such as each child of people born in Australia. Gifts to charities with accreditation from a state or national parliament exempt.

 Additional taxes so as to be same in all parts of Australia, with free trade among our 10 States.

 SPENDING AS A PROPORTION OF NATIONAL BUDGET REVENUE; Subject to the Treasurers budget passing both houses of Parliament; then spending submissions from the relevant minister shall to go to the state Citizens Juries and the Australian President to lend assent (reversible within 1 year).

90% of proceeds of sale of new currency coins and notes to be withdrawn from circulation.

Quantitative easing of 9% of gdp for equal monthly superannuation for citizens having less than GDP /

population then x 9. Other quantitative easing or government debt is illegal.

No borrowing or lending for existing (used) housing.

1;9% of revenue for one per household citizen fair skin mother for each fair skin dependant; child, husband, asset poor, disabled or aged. Including 18% superannuation contributions.

2;9% of revenue for welfare for productive asset poor fair complexion citizens over the age of 15years. Including 18% superannuation contributions. Not required waited or became disabled or unemployed. Proof of identity by DNA test, finger prints and photograph of face and accent test to prove Australian citizenship and born in Australia. Not required (optional) to provide documents to prove identity. Issue of bank account if did not have one. Compulsory voluntary work in advance for welfare at the rate of the minimum wage per hour; (by penalty of 18% assets test welfare reduction) for able unproductive fair skin citizens under the age of 50years to do work with private industry; for males in agriculture and building work; for females in cleaning and care homes or care for family; to receive; transport, accommodation, meals and protective clothing if for employer but no requirement on employers to pay a minimum wage.

3;9% of revenue for payment to extraterrestrials and time travellers for free videos to explain perpetual free ambient electron attraction electricity harvesting, anti-gravity, interstellar colonisation and time travel technologies; free to use technologies to commercialise in private research universities. To develop and provide free software {Linux}. For genetic engineering of humans, acquisition of extra terrestrial produce species and biological pest controls. For free private media including educational television channels to educate children and adults. Private medical research. Private microchip design.

4;9% of revenue private company to research and supply meal replacement nutritional supplements drink and antibody immunoglobulin (colostrum) free for all citizens who want it also for sale. {Each meals drink containing; 500mg ascorbic acid (vitamin c), 1gram omega 3 complex, 1gram magnesium complex, 1gram collagen, 1mg vitamin a complex, 2000iu vitamin d3, 50mg vitamin e complex, 1mg vitamin k complex, 20mg vitamin b1, 15mg vitamin b2, 20mg vitamin b3, 20mg vitamin b5, 20mg vitamin b6, 1mg vitamin b12, 1mg biotin, 2mg folic acid, 50mg inositol, 50mg choline, 400mg calcium, 20mg iron, 40mg phosphorous, 1mg iodine, 20mg zinc, 1mg selenium, 1mg copper, 5mg manganese, 1mg chromium, 1mg molybdenum, 100mg chloride, 1gram potassium complex, 1mg lithium, 500mg NAC. To consume with 2 eggs for breakfast, Vegetables, fruit and berries smoothie for lunch, and Dairy milk, turmeric, black pepper, garlic and ginger drink for dinner. Nut mix snacks.}

5;9% of revenue for to pay off private medical credit card debts after accessing superannuation medical savings investments each month of citizens from birth (and migrants after 15years probationary residency). Super funds shall invest in investments within Australia not in foreign nations; 36+% in own build rental and care home accommodation including hospitals such as in real estate investment trusts, 18+% for an industry for Australia to specialise in; {herbal and nutritional medicines and meal replacement drink powder}. [USA, Canada and Mexico; weapons and vehicles: China, Japan, Taiwan and Koreans microchip electronics: Britain; media and education: Russia region; energy: Scandinavia; genetics:] The superannuation account holder having a card to access to pay out pension of 1% of balance each month. The patient to pay 9% of medical treatments out of pocket [not 100% out of pocket for actual good treatments under Medicare; ambulance and specialist such as dentists and optical.] (out of pocket payment exempt for children to 20years of age and doctor to waiver if destitute) using debit account link of medical credit card and credit to pay for the balance medical treatments including nutritional medicines to automatically pay off each month from superannuation investments savings. The same charge for all patients (no boost because public purse). All patients must be given the price quote before voluntary acceptance of treatment or payment is optional. For to purchase; ambulance, emergency treatment, pharmaceuticals, tests, dental care, optical, disabled care, specialist, fertility services, immunotherapy and nutritional medicines; from private pharmacy chain, clinics, care homes and online health shop having accreditation. For private residential care homes for homeless or disabled including aged. Free fertility service payment for fair genetic material donor (white, red, orange blend skin; black, grey or yellow hair; and blue, green or brown eyes), collection for making of sperm cells if from men and egg cells if from females; for surrogates choice from 1,000 oldest males available and available females having 4 or more natural birth children; subject to genetic testing and choice by surrogate; plus for collection, fertilisation and implantation at private fertility clinics. The maximum pay of doctors is gdp / population then / 360 [$138] per treatment hour. Anyone may be a doctor (but for if disqualified) after passing clinic set test after 2 year as junior doctor under supervision of practicing doctor. Drug patents are illegal (all safe generics are legal). Costs of treatments for insured must be the same as out of pocket patients. Online pharmecies may sell medications direct to patients. All safe including experimental medications and treatments are legal. Ban on pharmecist or doctors indemnity insurance or malpractice compensation; pharmecists or doctors who harmed shall receive other penalties such as bans and prison.

6;9% of revenue for private contractors to build national free communications and transport infrastructure. Free wireless internet. Free electric self driving taxi pod buses. Free roads. Free railways.

7;9% of revenue for private contractors to construct national utilities and subdivision infrastructure. For subdivision roads, storm water drains, sewers, sewage works, water supply; dams. Plus base load power stations and power grid (illegal to connect to grid of intermittent electricity generators such as wind and solar); for privatisation and reinvestment of proceeds in more utilities and subdivision infrastructure. Plus building supplies companies to privatise.

8;9% of revenue for the Australian racist population policy. [Australians currently have the Constitutional right to deem necessary and for parliament to enact racist laws; 51xxvi] Payment to third countries to process and resettle black complexion people and refugees. Payment to black complexion people in exchange for voluntary sterilisation by injection. Banishment of black complexion natives to gender specific native title island prisons, deportation of black people. Free fertility services to produce pastel White, orange, red complexion, Yellow blonde, black, grey hair, and Blue, green, brown eyes children; voluntary election by males of and payment to fair complexion natural mothers to be female egg donor candidates, payment to males over age of 100 years sperm donor candidate (if required production of sperm from stem cells from somatic cells). Fair complexion mothers right to conceive from qualifying fair complexion sperm and egg donor candidate. No cloning. Human germ line genetic enhancements {genes to convert glucose to vitamin c, genes to convert omega 6 to omega 3}. For aid to independent (Papua New Guinea) for to accept those who have illegally invaded Australia, to process in open aid centres where illegals free to roam widely and go to their home nation of origin or ancestry. (Papua New Guinea) may force worst up to 90% to go home to nation of genetic ancestry and keep best 10% for more than 5 years. Border protection; within lands and territorial waters of Australia. No black complexion citizens, refugees or visitors and expulsion of those that have invaded including with aid to other nations including nation of genetic origin to resettle them. Right to migrate or travel to Australia is racist; only self reliant healthy male building and construction tradesmen and female super model wives; of white, red or orange complexion, black, grey or yellow hair, and brown, blue or green eyes, including time travellers and extra-terrestrials. Non citizens do not have citizens rights to vote, welfare, public housing, work in public service, medical subsidy, own land, or be heard by any court. Deportation of destitute non citizens reliant on free education, health care, homeless housing or food bank services. No foreign parents, refugees, tourists, students, doctors, farm workers, care staff or tattooed migrants or migrants who have been a member of an illegal religion {Islam}. Citizenship is by passing fair skin racial purity ancestry DNA test and by inheritance from fair skin father or after 15 years probation as good, productive and self reliant residents tolerant of our citizens bill of rights, then an English language proficiency test for full citizenship including for fair skin ancestry wife and children of any age. All guest visitors and migrants must pass AI facial recognition and DNA propensity test and blood test to be clean of infection before entry. Foreigners may own shares in companies listing on the public share market of Australia. Foreign illegals after 1 month or more in prison, then shall have free deportation to place of main genetic ancestry 1000+ years ago (using spit DNA test), so as to enforce their citizenship of nation of ethnic origin by any means with death penalty if refused to go or denied entry. Private militia may detain and deport black skin people and illegal migrants without court authorisation.

9;9% of revenue for governor generals military budget. For weapons including robots, drones, ordinance such as missiles and time travel; including for military aid. (No nuclear weapons) For emergency services vehicles. For private security video surveillance (including in public toilets). For private prisons. Also for customs, bio-security and border protection. Payment for inspections and disarmament of nuclear weapons.

10;9% of revenue for national, state and local government spending; private companies for infrastructure maintenance, rubbish bin emptying and infrastructure maintenance, free public zoos and botanic gardens under private management.

Private company to remove all normal single reflection reversed image mirrors that made people insane; and replacement with true image video monitors and reflection of reflection true image mirror pairs at slightly acute of right angle in corner; so read writing in image correctly; (not reversed); so make people sane and care for self properly. Private regulator to ban toxic agricultural chemicals and food ingredients. 9% of this budget to spend an equal salary per year for government officials; members of parliament, local councils, the citizens jury and staff.

11;9% of revenue to pay private builders to build free private single room boarding shelters (with fridge, washing machine and furniture) and pay private shelters to provide 3 daily meals, air conditioning, weekly cleaning and care for disabled; for fair skin citizens born in the state with least gross assets who do not have family to live with;

Bill Of Rights:

Citizens born in the nation shall have these rights; (Also for time travellers and extra terrestrials)

The right to; True images of self such as live television selfies not single reflection reversed images (right to be sane). Freedom to believe, tell and know the truth (what woke, state media, racist blacks or deviants said was disinformation, wrong or hate) except other peoples passwords; and not indoctrinated gender fraud (transsexualism), homosexual propaganda, bigoted unfair black racist voices or flags; or fiction or promoted other degenerate vices or communicated weapons of mass indiscriminate destruction designs. Verbally vilify black skin people for have unfairly physically physically savaged, imposed tyranny or robbed, and have private security police prison black savages; who were violently offended by the truth and hatred; with lethal force if necessary. Free home schooling educational television not violent fiction. Copy technology free of patent restrictions or fee. Be safe in public; be on private security video surveillance, including in public toilets. Not be bombarded with unwanted advertising. Change thy name. Deem necessary and enact racist laws; only to favour fair complexion races and not to allocate racist budget funding only to dark complexion races. Free open access wireless internet, free software. Industry sponsorship of free industry skills video libraries. Right to repair (products must be easily repairable by the user or have 10year warranty for free collection, repair and delivery by maker). Simple easy taxation and laws. Have a bank account at any local bank branch. Invest in any venture; not restricted to wealthy sophisticated investors. Use commercially any peaceful technology free of restriction such as by patent holders. If convicted sentencing by a random jury of 10 fair citizens not panel of judges who by 5 largest party appointment shall just conduct the trial. Permanent affordable single story housing adequate to raise a fair family if female, with workshop if male. Individual own bedroom. Live with family when paying board of 36% of income after tax to female carer such as wife, mother or daughter. Free use of rain water falling on own or rental property. Support to wives and mothers for each dependant. For tenants to have a free temporary or permanent guest such as a fair partner and fair children. Not be evicted when paying the maximum rent per tenant of 36% of the welfare payment for asset poor, except where agreeing with compensation for the tenant; (may evict free guests or if not paying 36% of standard assets test welfare as rent). Leave a rental property at any time, without notice and free of penalty; only compensating landlord for damaged rental property when staying. Clear, subdivide, develop (but not build multiple stories except in central business district), redevelop and have industry on own land free of government impediment; subject only to solid construction (no plasterboard walls), standard roads and utility infrastructure requirements. Free rubbish collection and disposal. Where over the age of 15 years; heterosexually harass to a reasonable extent and have sex by mutual consent without retribution. Female to choose sperm and egg fair donor, genetic testing, genetic engineering, fertility and birthing services. Manage own assets and finances. Life and if disabled to die only if wanted to. Buy, have and consume nutritional medicines. Immune therapy if had cancer not other toxic drugs. Have nutritional supplements and medicines including in hospitals and care homes. Refuse medical treatment free of penalty. Choice of healthy food, not toxic, not had carbohydrates, trans fats or inflammatory oils. Be cool in summer and warm in winter. Exercise. Work free of coercion, slavery or penalty; with free of charge on site meals, transport to work and if employer provides; accommodation. Employ when paying the minimum wage; without paying for leave or redundancy. Care and shelter if homeless and asset poor; without required became black, unemployed, disabled or aged. Drive (unless disqualified) free of (license or registration) fee, fine, insurance or compensation, only requiring free vision test and written road rules test every 4 years (no driving test). Discriminate only in favour of good virtue propensity identities such as Truth, White, orange or red complexion, Yellow blonde, black or grey hair, Blue, green or brown eyes, Young, Sexist, English speaking, Right name, Strait sexuality, Able, Asset poor, Hygienic, Intelligent, Sane, Beautiful, Clean, Peaceful, and Local products, nationality, language and culture; and only discriminate against bad savagery propensity identities such as Lied, Black complexion, Aged, Asset rich, Feminist (misandrist), Multicultural, Wrong name, Fraudulent gender, Disabled, Infected, Stupid, Insane, Ugly, Dirty, Violent, and Foreign nationality, language and culture.

Fair complexion citizens born in the nation shall not have these rights;

Contraception. Abortion (except where the fetus had genetic defect such had black skin). Conception and sex with black skin people.

Dark complexion people shall have these additional rights; Voluntary contraceptive sterilisation and abortion with compensation. Native title prison islands. Payback and other tribal law between blacks (not inflicted on whites). Play contact sport. Grow, make, import and consume intoxicants such as alcohol and drugs in native title prison islands.

Dark complexion savages shall not have these rights;

Migrate to, enter, retain citizenship of, reside in or have any case on behalf of be heard in any court of Australia. Possess guns. Written or oral voice or to be heard in media. Conception and sex with fair skin people. Own land (black aboriginal native title is void). Compensation and reparations. Public housing. Schools, technical colleges and universities. Steal (fish, hunt or harvest) wild or fair skin farmer produce.

Cultural vices which are illegal;

The manufacture, sale or consumption of alcohol or other drugs that intoxicated. Virtual images (normal single reflection mirror back to front images); that made insane. Gambling (except on share market). Fiction. Gender fraud. Homosexuality or homosexual and transgender propaganda and marriage. Unhygienic daily shaving (may shave every 6 months). Personal gun or weapon ownership. Racist black laws, selection criteria, land rights, royalties, welfare, mobs, violence, looting, vandalism, graffiti, art, organisations, media, and voices. Smoking and vaping. Lied in accused men of rape or violently or financially assaulted men falsely accused of rape. Debt. Sun tanning. Makeup. Jewellery, Fashion (only allowing national colour code). Art. Sculpture. Tattoos. Gangs. Unions. Hobbies. Collecting. Toys. Pets. Cartoons, animations and video games (only allowing simulators). Sugar, other carbohydrates, salt, trans fats or fried foods. Insurance. Free imports (free trade). Socialism; paid public service (except by constitutional election or random selection). Communism; publicly owned industry, education, hospitals and media (except transport and water infrastructure). Welfare for working asset poor is legal. Multiculturalism. Qualifications except tests for potential employees the employer may do. Pharmaceutical drugs except may have nutritional medicines, herbs and antibodies.

Fair males shall have this work and education: Heavy engineering, building trades and maintenance, garbage collection, military, police, agriculture, mechanic, mining, policy, banking, business management, scientist, inventor, Teacher of males. Inheritance from male ancestors including uncles. Sport.

Fair females shall have this work and education: Family care; child, disabled and aged care, Aid worker, Nurse, Doctor, Textiles, Sales, Receptionist, Precision manufacturing. Dietitian, Laundry, Cleaning, Fertility, Cook, Mother, Teacher of females. Mothers welfare recipient. Inheritance from female ancestors including aunts. Music. Dance.

Both males and females shall have this education and these jobs: Politics. Speaker.

Writer. Investor. Driver. Video maker. Photographer.

Commandments And Directives:

Thou shall not kill except to save good, fair and true life; Thou shall not worship reverse or virtual or cartoon or any other reverse images such as of normal single reflection mirror; Thou shall only contemplate designs and true images of self and world such as on television, video and of reflection of reflection slightly acute of right angle mirror pairs in corner configuration so view from centre of room to see only true images. Thou porn shall be of all fair complexion heterosexual partners. Thou shall communicate good of self and future or bad of past or others. Thou shall price products in value of silver per ounce standard measure (with 100 silver ounces equal to 1 gold ounce). Thou shall not alter any part of property paying rent for and shall only cover mirrors or chrome so not reflected. Thou shall be friends with neighbours. Thou shall only talk to the landlord when the landlord asks for a response. Thou shall have rest from physical work every second day and do only free charity work on Sundays. Thou shall marry on impregnation to remain together as a family as long as children shall live, Thou garden shall have only food produce trees such as of fruit and nuts and food egg layer; except shall reserve 10% of property for natural species biodiversity; Thou shall eat healthiest supplements and foods first. Thou shall not deploy toxic chemicals such as agricultural pesticides or domestic bug spray and shall not insert toxic chemical genes in food and shall only eliminate pests with biological controls, contraceptives and gun not toxic poisons; Thou shall be in shade from sun while having face and hands visible as much as is healthy; Thou shall wear locally made clothes and eat locally grown food and buy products of local manufacture; Thou shall not wear high or narrow heels or wear make up or spray tan or camouflage paint; Thou shall not normally eat meat at home, only away from home or in emergencies, (may consume unsweetened gelatin (collagen), eggs and milk).

Thou shall make sell and buy in quantities and factors of the the natural number of the thing (below) x 1, 2, 10, 20, 100, 200,,,,, kilograms and for dry product containers and litres for liquids for example.

The nature of numbers;

(also in multiples of 2 and 10)

1-Enterprise; the power of 1 to design.

2-Life; the power of 2 to evolve.

3-Food; 3 meals each day.

4-Vehicles; 4, 8 and 16 wheels.

5-Dwellings; Walls plus roof.

6-Electric power; 6 cells in battery, bank of 6 batteries, 6 batteries charger, 6 volts.

7-Words; 7 letters in word, 7 words in sentence, 7 sentences in paragraph, 7 paragraphs in chapter, 7 chapters in part section, 7 part sections in book for example.

8-Computer; (example) 8gb ram, 8 cores, 800gb storage memory.

9-Money; price of $9.

10-Decimal system.

11-Work teams such as of male volunteers and female workers for pay.

12-Produce trees and livestock; 12chickens 12nut and fruit trees. Carton of dozen eggs.

The meaning (purpose) of life is to cross fertilise female care and beauty with male wealth and longevity. The purpose of the nature (Gaia) is to create time travel to go back in time to seed the universe including time to create this same universe to be best for us doing this. Join say 2x 1.8meter tall x 75cm wide good quality glass mirrors by duct tape up outside of junction of one long edge so each pair (2) mirrors are face to face. These 2 mirrors will then self stand when slightly acute of right angle so fit in corners of room so 2 pairs; a pair of 2 in opposite corners so have true images feedback; for strategic self defence capabilities. No virtual images (back to front normal single reflection rear vision mirror as had writing was back to front) either as good felt bad so was abused or raped or destroyed or killed by bad or bad felt empowerment so abused, raped, destroyed or killed good. Selfie smartphone and computers must have matte screen and true image selfies not back to front selfie view.

ALPHABET; vowels round and consonants strait font.

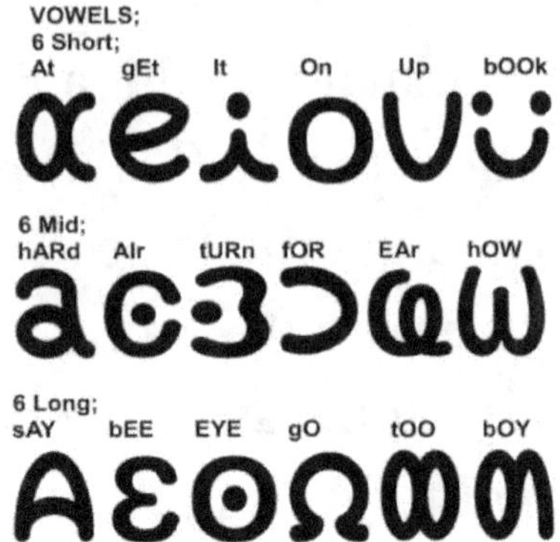

UNIVERSAL NAMING CODE; [update]

3 Consonants groups;

Back; H, Ng, R, Y, G, K, Ch, J.

Pallet; viSion, Sh, Z, S, N, D, L, T.

Front; THe, THing, F, V, M, W, B, P.

3 Vowels groups;

Short; At, bEd, It, Of, Up, bOOk.

Mid; fAR, AIr, hER, fOR, EAr, cOW.

Long; Ate, EAt, I, gO, tOO, bOY.

Consonants;
Places; Best; first front, middle pallet, last back.

Neutral; first back, middle front, last pallet.
Worst; first pallet, middle back, last front.
Products; Best; first pallet, middle back, last front.
Neutral; first front, middle pallet, last back.
Worst; first back, middle front, last pallet.
Species; Best; first back, middle front, last pallet.
Neutral; first pallet, middle back, last front.
Worst; first front, middle pallet, last back.
Male; Best; first front, middle back, last pallet.
Neutral; first back, middle pallet, last front.
Worst; first pallet, middle front, last back.
Female; Best; firsts pallet, middle front, last back.
Neutral; first front, middle back, last pallet.
Worst; first back, middle pallet, last front.
Surname; Best; first back, middle pallet, last front.
Neutral; first pallet, middle front, last back.
Worst; first front, middle back, last pallet.
Vowels;
Male; Best; first short, last long.
Neutral; first mid, last short.
Worst; first long, last mid.
Female; Best; first mid, last long.
Neutral; first long, last short.
Worst; first short, last mid.
Surname; Best; first long, last short.
Neutral; first short, last mid.
Worst; first mid, last long.
Places; Best; first short, last mid.
Neutral; first mid, last long.

Worst; first long, last short.
Products; Best; first long, last mid.
Neutral; first short, last long.
Worst; first mid, last short.
Species; Best; first mid, last short.
Neutral; first long, last mid.
Worst; first short, last long.
UNIVERSAL COLOUR CODE: [to improve]

White; tools, white goods and appliances; washing machine, toilet, basin, fridge, blender, vacuum cleaner, microwave oven, stove, air conditioner (heating and cooling), cutlery, lamp, lighting. Toothbrush. Industrial tools, robots, vehicles and drones. Industrial hand tools. Desk, bed and chair (fabric green) Container; bowl, cup. Cupboards.

Grey; Rubber feet of appliances and tools. Wheels, tyres. Footwear both genders; socks, boots. Pants both genders; shorts, skirt, trousers, jeans, belt (pants).

Black; Information technology; television, printer, computer, smartphone, wrist watch, pen. Reading glasses.

Brown; Building exterior. Exterior doors and window frames.

Red (pink, bright red and dark red); Female upper long winter over warm clothing; coat, hat.

Orange; Male long warm upper over clothes; jacket, hat.

Yellow (light yellow, bright yellow and gold); Buildings interior, ceiling, and floor. Interior doors and window frames.

Green; Linen; Bedding fabric; (blanket, quilt cover, sheets, pillow, sleeping bag, seating fabric). Towel, hanky, tissue, toilet paper. Curtains. Carpet. Luggage; backpack, wallet.

Blue (light blue, royal blue and navy blue); Male upper summer under shade clothes; shirt, hat.

Purple (lilac purple, deep purple); Female upper summer under shade clothes; short sleeve shirt, hat.

Clear; Window,

Background; Doors.

Image; Image; video screens.

Natural; Food.

Black, grey, yellow; Hair.

White, red, orange, purple; Complexion, teeth, eye balls, veins.

Brown, blue, green; Eyes iris.

Private security police and military shall arrest and remand illegals, violent, intoxicated, or other criminals subject to judgement of the local court or Governor General tribunal. Each prisoner to have own cell with shower, toilet, basin, drinking water, fresh air with temperature control, built in bed, storage, power point for electric blanket, built in table measuring more than 1m by 2m with power points for television and lamp, secure door and ceiling. No hanging points.

Private security police and military shall deport illegals and banish blacks to native title areas; to allow blacks to meat out tribal justice between each other.

The Governor General shall set laws for governance of our external protectorates and territories as the President shall allocate.

Location of Parliaments, Local council chambers, Reserve Bank, and all national infrastructure. Shall be as the Governor General determines on advice from the Prime Minister, Premiers, ministers and Mayors subject to funding and construction within 5 years.

Swearing in oath of affirmation: {I, [name] do solemnly and sincerely affirm and declare that I will be faithful and bear true allegiance to the fair President according to law. SO HELP ME GOD!}

All information between {} brackets is set by a majority of a joint sitting of both houses of the national parliament unless otherwise indicated. All information between [] brackets is comment and has no legal effect on the constitution. All information between () brackets has the same consequence as the rest of the text.

www.ingramcontent.com/pod-product-compliance
Lightning Source LLC
Chambersburg PA
CBHW060208260726
48658CB00005BA/1947